PYTHON:

THE NO-BULLSH*T

GUIDE

Learn Python Programming Within 12 Hours!

CYBERPUNK UNIVERSITY

Table of Contents

which are incurred as a result of the use of information contained within this document, including, but not limited to, —errors, omissions or inaccuracies.

Introduction

You have made the right first stride towards becoming a hobbyist or a professional programmer using Python, one of the most widely used programming language on computers today. First off, welcome to a presentation of Cyberpunk University. Thank you for investing in this book, and we hope you will follow through it to learn how to develop your coding skills and become a Python programmer with ease within just days.

This book is structured into 12 practical chapters that take roughly an hour to do. We have designed the content of the book to be easy to follow for both complete beginners to programming and those with knowledge of other programming languages or have been introduced to Python partially before. The over 50 exercises distributed over the 12 hours of the course duration are an excellent way to get started learning to master all the essentials about Python.

Cyberpunk University is committed to producing content that helps learners discover their coding skills and to learn processes that make it easy for them to think of solutions to daily human problems. Many other programming books are coming in the future so be sure to check our catalog and get the chance to learn even more ways to write programs in different languages that computers can understand.

To help you get the most out of this book we have created the **FREE** "**Cyberpunk Python Whizz Kit**". The Kit contains an awesome cheat sheet to help you program as fast as possible and we've also included **ALL** the exercises from this book in python files. You can use them however you want.

DOWNLOAD THE FREE WHIZZ KIT HERE:

subscribe.cyberpunkuniversity.com

Hour 1: Getting Started with Python

Whether this is your initial foray into the world of programming, or learning Python to expand your programming skills set with a new language, you have come to the right place.

Every programmer has a story about they got into programming and what the first program they wrote was. This book is intended for complete beginners in the world of programming and Python in particular, and we hope it will be useful enough for you to remember it when you tell the story of your path to being a successful professional or hobbyist programmer in the future.

This book focuses more on the practical aspects of writing code in Python. You do not need external resources to master the basics of Python programming, although some people find extensive researching useful. If you are a beginner in programming, I would recommend that you follow this guide EXACTLY as instructed and only venture to wider research and practice after you understand the concepts each chapter teaches. This will help prevent the confusion that arises from taking instructions from different sources.

This book is structured to guide you learn the essential basics of Python programming in 12 hours, each chapter representing an hour of code.

1.1 What is Python?

Everyone today knows what a computer is and understand why programmers are responsible for computers (including machines, Smartphone, cars, planes, etc.) do what we 'command' them to do. By learning to program, you have chosen to join the millions of programmers who strive to make life easier by writing programs in a computer language that instruct machines what to do. Python is one of these programs.

We can define Python as a very popular high-level, general-purpose, interpreted, and dynamic programming language that is very easy to learn. The design philosophy of Python focuses on code readability, and its syntax makes it easy for programmers to express the concepts in a computer program in fewer lines of code compared to other popular languages such as Java and C++.

1.2 Top Benefits of Learning Python Programming

Python is a general-purpose programming language. This means when you become a Python programmer, you can build just about anything from website back-end and artificial intelligence systems to desktop apps and robotic programs.

Besides, because of its code readability, Python is very easy to understand and can be a perfect Launch pad for individuals hoping to go ahead and learn other more complicated languages. The language is governed by flexible rules, it offers limitless career opportunities to those who master it as a skill, and to put it simply, Python is the programming language of the future.

There is also a very vibrant and active support community with ready answers to all questions and concerns you will have during and after learning. StackOverflow and Github are the best examples. The vibrant Python community is always willing to share means that most tools and libraries you will need to make your work easy will be just a click away.

1.3 Minimum Requirements

To make use of this book, you must meet a few requirements:

1.   Python is a cross-platform language. You must have a computer running Windows, Mac, or Linux operating system.

2. You must pay attention to detail. What typically separates good programs from bad ones is how meticulous they are in recognizing every element in the code, from a comma to space.

3. You must have basic computer skills. This means you should be able to download and install a program, type, manipulate files on your computer, and know how to read and write (duh!).

1.4 Installing Python and Text Editor

Installing Python is simple. The most recent version of Python (Python 3.5) is often included in many UNIX and Linux distributions.

Step 1: On your browser, go to www.python.org. Hover your pointer over the Download button and click Python 3.5.2 to download for your operating system. You will also need to know whether your operating system is 32-bit or 64-bit to download the correct version.

Fig 1.1 Downloading Python

If you need assistance at this point there is an invaluable resource for beginners on https://wiki.python.org/moin/BeginnersGuide.

You will also notice there are two versions of Python: an older version 2.7.12 and the newer version 3.5. Both are available for download, but in this book, we will be using Python 3.5.2. The beginner's guide above explains the difference between the two.

Step 2: Wait for the download to complete then run the installation.

Fig 1.2: Installing Python

By default, Python installs to a directory on root with a name with version number embedded. For instance, if you are using Windows, your program should install in C:\Python35-32\. You can change install location by clicking 'Customize installation'.

Step 3: Check the 'Add Python 3.5 to PATH option and complete the installation. Leave all other options as-is. Once an installation is complete, you will be able to write Python code as instructed in this book and run the code using an interactive interpreter that it is bundled with. With the interpreter, you will be able to type commands line by line and see the results immediately, hence experiment further and learn faster.

You can start the Python Shell by clicking on the Python IDLE link in the shortcut installation directly such as the desktop, dock or start menu. You should see something like this:

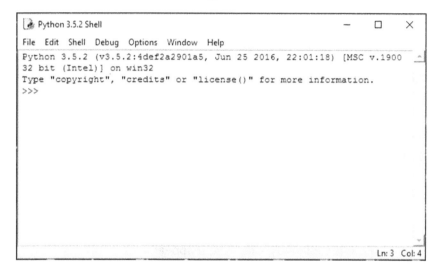

Fig 1.3 Python Shell

Step 4: Create a folder inside the Python installation location to save your Python programs and name it 'ExFiles.' If you followed the instructions during setup and installed Python in C:\Python35-32\, then your practice files will be saved in C:\Python35-32\ExFiles\. This will be substantial in executing your scripts.

1.4.1 Alternative Text Editors

A good text editor is a must-have accessory if you look forward to being a good developer. Most text editors available on the internet have all the necessary tools you need to create and manage notes, write down notes or just provide distraction-free coding. You cannot use word processors such as MS Word to write your code. The top 5 text editors with a free version that you can download and try are:

- Sublime Text (My favorite)
- Notepad++
- Vim (and its variations)
- Atom
- Text Wrangler (for Mac).

Personally, I prefer Sublime Text. For this course, you can use Notepad++ if you want a simple but powerful editor you can get used to.

1.5 Hello World! Your First Program

To write your first program:

1. Start Python Shell.

2. Type the following exactly as it appears:

```
Print ("Hello World")
```

Fig 1.4 Hello Worlds!

Press Enter.

This is what you should see:

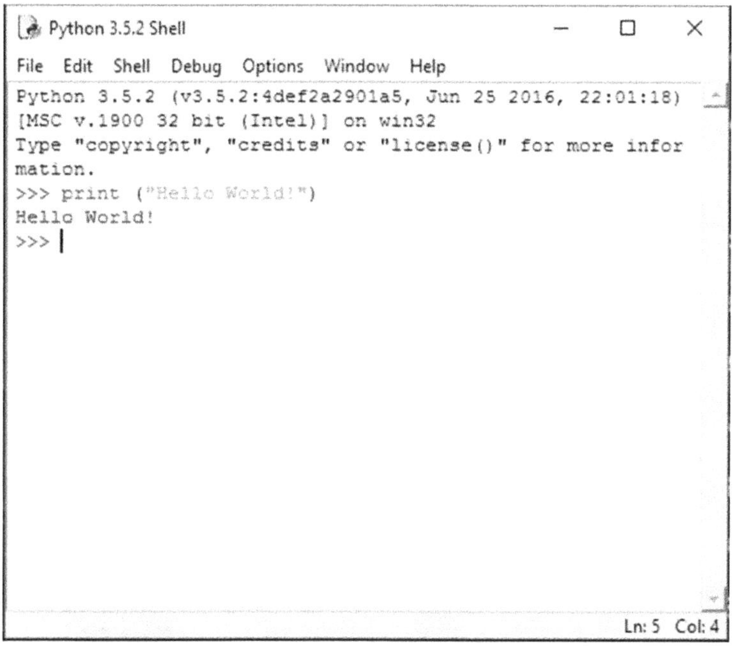

```
Python 3.5.2 Shell                                    —    □    ×

File  Edit  Shell  Debug  Options  Window  Help
Python 3.5.2 (v3.5.2:4def2a2901a5, Jun 25 2016, 22:01:18)
[MSC v.1900 32 bit (Intel)] on win32
Type "copyright", "credits" or "license()" for more infor
mation.
>>> print ("Hello World!")
Hello World!
>>> |



                                                        Ln: 5  Col: 4
```

Fig 1.5 Hello World!

Save the file as HelloWorld.py in the 'ExFiles' directory you created during setup. Save the file by clicking 'File' then 'Save As.' Remember to type the name is including the '.py.' Extension each time. In this case, name your file "HelloWorld.py" then click 'Save.'

Congratulations! You are now a Python Programmer!

1.6 Running saved .py files

As I mentioned in Exercise 1, Python scripts are stored with an extension .py. Throughout this book, you follow coding instructions and save files before you can run them, unlike in exercise 1. In this section, I will show you how to run the Hello World! Program you saved in Exercise 1 to show you what to do in every other exercise in this book.

To run the python scripts you will create during this course, and you will need to learn a few things about the command line. The instructions are pretty much the same for all platforms – Windows Power Shell and Linux and Mac Terminals.

Step 1: Start the command terminal (Powershell/Terminal) and type Python. On Mac, place a shortcut to your terminal on the dock for easier access.

In Windows, the Command Prompt should look like this:

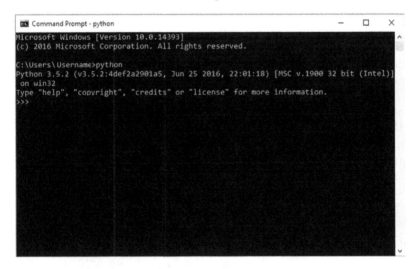

Fig 1.6: Windows Command Prompt

Step 2: You can run Python by typing the word Python on your command line. Try it.

To quit python and return to the terminal program, press Ctrl+Z (^Z).

Step 3: To run a Python script you saved in ExFiles folder, you will learn to go to the directory on the command line. First, quit python by pressing Ctrl+Z then type "cd.." and press to move a level up and again till you are on the root of your drive.

Step 4: Change directory to ExFiles by typing "cd C:\Python35-32\ExFiles."

Step 5: To run the HelloWorld.py script you saved in ExFiles, while on the terminal, type:

"Python HelloWorld.py"

You will be using this process to execute the exercise scripts you will code while we progress with this course. You will get used to these steps.

Quiz

Q: In this chapter, you learned that Python is an interpreted language. What does that mean?

A: Just like with PHP, Python's code is processed at runtime. No external program is needed to compile the code before running it.

Q: Why is Python considered a beginner's language?

A: Python's code is readable, and it is an easy language to learn. It also supports the development of a great selection of applications.

Hour 2: Variables, Strings and Basic Data Types

2.1 Variables

Variables are reserved memory spaces that store values. Simply put, when you create a variable, you reserve some memory space to store certain values.

The Python interpreter determines the memory be allocated and the data to be stored in it depending on the values you assign the variables. By assigning different data types to the variables, the interpreter reserves spaces for integers, decimals, or characters.

2.1.1 How to assign values to variables

Variables are automatically declared when you assign a value to a variable using the equal sign (=) such that variable = value. For instance, in my_age=22, the variable my_age has a value of 22.

Ex1

Start your editor and enter the following Python code:

Be careful not to miss the commas or misspell the variable names. You should see something like this:

```
#Ex1

product_ID = 10 #Integer assignment

product_price = 2.5 #float assignment

product_name = "Soda" #String assignment


print (product_ID)

print (product_price)

print (product_name)
```

In this exercise, you assign the variables product_ID, product_price, and product_namedifferent values then command the interpreter to display those values. If you get an error, check and re-check your spelling and commas and ensure everything is EXACTLY as it appears. The result should look like this:

```
C:\Python35-32\Exfiles>python Ex1.py
10
2.5
Soda

C:\Python35-32\Exfiles>
```

Do not worry about the types of assignments. We will discuss them later in the book.

2.1.2 Multiple variable assignments

When dealing with several related variables, you can assign one value to some variables simultaneously e.g.

```
x = y = z = 2
```

In this example, the integer value 2 is created and the variables x, y and z are assigned to the integer memory location. You can also assign multiple variables different values at a go. For example, in exercise 2, we could have easily assigned the variables as follows:

 example, in exercise 2, we could have easily assigned the variables as follows:

```
product_ID, product_price, product_name = 10, 2.5,
"Soda"
```

The variables product_ID, product_price, and product_name are assigned values 10, 2.5, and "Soda" respectively.

2.2 Standard Data Types

Python has five standard types of data that define operations that can be carried out on them as well as how they are stored in memory. They five data types we will cover in this section are:

- Numbers
- Strings
- Lists
- Tuples
- Dictionary
- Comments

2.2.1 Numbers

Numbers are essential numeric values that are created when a value is assigned to them. For instance, when you create a variable my_age and assign it a value of 22, the number 22 is created. There are three different types of numbers you will be working with:

Integers (int) – These are long integers e.g. 1, -12, 02.00, 372, 18374, -1862, -0x260, 100000,

Floats (float) – These are numbers with decimal points e.g. 1.0, 0.5, -734.2, 13.90201, 32.3+e18, -32.54e100, 0490

Complex – How complex do 3.14j, 45.j, 9.322e-36j, 876j, -.6545+0J, 3e+26J, 4.53e-7j look? These are numbers with ordered pairs of real floating-point numbers written x + yj where j is an imaginary unit.

In the next chapter, we will divulge deeper into numbers and even use various operators to manipulate them.

2.2.2 Strings

Think of these as plain characters within single or double quotation marks. You will get used to strings a lot. A string is created by enclosing text and numbers in either single or double quotes and can be declared with a star.

Start Python Shell and enter the following string operations to see what they do:

```
#Ex2

str1 = "Hello World!"


print (str1)          #Displays the entire string contents

print (str1[0])             #Displays the first character
in a string

print (str1[2:])            #Displays from the 5th
character in a string

print (str1*3)              #Displays the string content 3
times

print (str1[1:3])   #Displays characters 2 to 3 in a
string

print ("Testing", str1)     #Displays a concatenated
string.
```

Here is what you should see when you run the script.

```
Hello World!

H

llo World!

Hello World!Hello World!Hello World!

el

Testing Hello World!
```

2.2.3 Lists

A list contains separate items enclosed within square brackets [ ] and are separated by commas. The values on a list can be accessed using the same slice operators [ ] and [:] just like with strings. Also, just as with strings, the + sign is the concatenation while the * is the repletion operation symbol.

Ex3

Start your code editor and enter the following code as it appears:

```
#Ex3

fruits_list = ["oranges", "bananas", "peaches",
"mangoes"]

vegs_list = ["kales", "cabbages"]


print (fruits_list)          #Displays the entire list of
fruits_list

print (fruits_list[0])            #Displays the first
item in the list

print (fruits_list[2:4])   #Displays items 3 through 5
in the list

print (vegs_list * 3)             #Displays the list
three times

print (fruits_list[1:])           #Displays item 2
onwards

print (fruits_list[:2])           #Displays all items
to the third

print (vegs_list + fruits_list)#Displays concatenated
list
```

The result should look like this:

```
Command Prompt                                    —  □  ✕

C:\Python35-32\Exfiles>python Ex3.py
['oranges', 'bananas', 'peaches', 'mangoes']
oranges
['peaches', 'mangoes']
['kales', 'cabbages', 'kales', 'cabbages', 'kales', 'cabbages']
['bananas', 'peaches', 'mangoes']
['oranges', 'bananas']
['kales', 'cabbages', 'oranges', 'bananas', 'peaches', 'mangoes']
C:\Python35-32\Exfiles>_
```

2.2.4 Tuples

Tuples are a lot like lists in that they are sequential data. It is made up of values separated by commas and enclosed in parentheses (). The main difference between lists and tuples (besides one using square brackets and the other parentheses) is that the items defined in a file can be changed (updated) while those in tuples cannot. The operations on tuples are similar to those of lists.

25

Ex4

```
#Ex4

tup_1 = ('London', 2017, '$20.00', 5.2, "x")

tup_2 = (60,"magic",2017,"5.0")


print (tup_1[0], tup_2)

print (tup_2, tup1[1:3])

print (tup_2*2)
```

Like strings and lists, tuple indices start at 0 and can be concatenated, sliced, and so on.

2.2.5 Dictionaries

In Python, a dictionary is a kind of hash table type that works like associative arrays with key-value pairs and enclosed in curly braces { }. A dictionary can be almost any type of Python data but typically contains numbers and strings. Values are often any arbitrary Python objects.

Ex5

Dictionaries

```
#Ex5

dict_1 = {"one"}

dict_2 = {"John", "Sales", 87255, "come home")


print ("This is dictionary number ", dict_1[0])

print (dict_2.keys())
```

Dictionaries do not have any concept of order when it comes to elements and can be said to be unordered or simply "out of order." In hour 7, we will look at dictionaries more exhaustively.

2.2.6 Comments

Comments are not particularly a data type, but every programming language needs because they are essential to human developers. Comments, marked by the pound or hash character, are used to tell the human reader what something means or does in English.

They are also used to disable parts of the program when you need to remove them temporarily. The best example of using comments is demonstrated in Ex3 you did in this chapter. Note that Python ignores everything in a line of code beginning with the #. In fact, your text editor should color comments differently to show you which characters will be ignored.

Hour 3: User Input, Basic Math, and Output

Every computer program is written to solve a user problem, and as such, it must accept some form of input from the user. In most cases, the input is through the keyboard. For this purpose, Python provides the input() function to input data. The prompt string is an optional input parameter you can learn about later.

3.1 input ()

The program flow ill stop until the user enters the expected data and press enter when the input function is called. The text of the optional character may be displayed on the screen.

The input the user entered is returned as a string without modification. Other functions such as casting and eval can be later used to transform the data into a different type as per the algorithm.

Ex5

Input

Write the following code:

```
#Ex5

name = input("What is your name: ")

age = input("How old are you?: ")

location = input("Where do you live?: ")


print ("You are ", name, "from", location, "and
you are", age, "years old.")
```

Save the script in your practice files folder and run it. This is what you should see:

```
name = input("What is your name: ")

What is your name: John

age = input("How old are you?: ")

How old are you?: 22

location = input("Where do you live?: ")

Where do you live?: London


print ("You are ", name, "from", location, "and you
are", age, "years old.")

You are John from London and you are 22 years old.
```

3.2 More Numbers

Considering that numbers are immutable data types, changing the value of an assigned number data type will result in a newly allocated object. This also means that when assign a value to a number object, a new one is created. For instance:

```
distance = 100

time = x = 6


x = int(input ("Time in seconds: "))

speed = distance / time
```

Example 3.2

In the above example, the value that the user enters will replace the value of x which is 6.

3.2.1 Number Type Conversion

Before you can begin working with numbers, you must know how to convert from one type to another. The most typical conversion is converting strings to integers and floats and converting between floats and integers. These are what you need to know now.

In example 3.2, because the user input is a string by default, we used int() to convert it to an integer before we can calculate speed. Python converts expressions with mixed data types internally. The expressions employed in the conversion are:

- To convert x to a plain integer type int(x)
- To convert x to a floating-point number type float(x)
- To convert x to a complex number with real part x type complex(x)

3.2.2 Basic Math Operators

Every programming language needs to have a way of calculating numbers and math to make it useful. This section deals a lot about symbols. You are probably already familiar with the operation symbols you will use to carry out comparisons and calculations because they are standard:

+ plus (add)

- minus (subtract)

/ slash (divide)

* asterisk (multiply)

< less than

> greater than

<= less than or equal

>= greater than or equal

% percent

Ex6

Let us use these symbols in this exercise. Code the following:

```
#Ex6
print ("Now I will count my fruits")

mangoes = 6 + 8+2
apples = 9 / 3 + 1
peaches = 4 * 3 - 2

print ("Mangoes", mangoes)
print ("Apples", apples)
print ("Peaches", peaches)

print ("How many fruits have I eaten?")
mangoes_left = int(input ("How many mangoes are
left?"))
apples_left = int(input ("How many apples are
left?"))
peaches_left = int(input ("How many peaches are
left?"))

#Now let us calculate the number of fruits eaten
mangoes_eaten = mangoes - mangoes_left
apples_eaten = apples - apples_left
peaches_eaten = peaches - peaches_left

print ("You have eaten ", mangoes_eaten,
"mangoes,", apples_eaten, "apples, and ",
peaches_eaten, "peaches.")
```

In this exercise, first we use random numbers to calculate how many fruits we have then we display

In this exercise, first, we use random numbers to calculate how many fruits we have then we display it. The program then prompts for input (integers) of the number of fruits left which it uses to calculate how many we have eaten. Follow each line of code to understand what it does and where you could improve fully.

3.2.1 Comparison Operators

So far we have looked at and used mathematical operators. Python allows you to compare values on either side of an equation and decides how they relate. Here is a breakdown of these relational operators:

==	equal	The condition becomes true if the values of two operands are equal	(x == y)
!=	not equal	The condition becomes true if the values of two operands are not equal	(x != y)
>	Greater than	The condition becomes true if the value of the left operand is greater than that of the right	(x > y)
<	Less than	The condition becomes true if the value of the left operand is less than that of the right	(x < y)
>=	Greater than or equal	The condition becomes true if the value of the left operand is equal to or greater than of the right	(x >= y)
<=	Less than or equal	The condition becomes true if the value on the left operand is equal to or less than that of the right	(x <= y)

Ex7

```
#Ex7

#Program to determine whether a shape is a
rectangle or a square and calculate its area
and perimeter.

height = float(input("Enter the height of the
shape: "))

length = float(input("Enter the width of the
shape: "))


if (height == length):

      shape = "square"

else:

      shape = "rectangle"


area = (height * length)

perimeter = ((length + height)*2)


print ("The shape is a", shape, "with an area
of ", area, "and perimeter of ", perimeter,".")
```

Can you change the data types for height and length to integer and
see what answers you get?

Precedence	Operation	Definition
Highest	()	Anything in parentheses is computed first.
	**	Exponentiation
	-x, +x	Negation
	*, /, %, //	Multiplication, division, modulo,
	+, -	Addition, subtraction
	<, >, <=, >=, !=, ==	relational operators
	not	Logical
	and	Logical
Lowest	or	Logical

3.2.3 Order of Operations

It is a good practice always to indicate the order of operations when writing expressions in Python using parentheses (). If you do not, Python applies the standard order of operations you know from Algebra and Geometry in high school. Mathematical operations are evaluated in this PEMDAS order:

Ex8

```
#Ex8
#Example 1
x = 87 / 3 * 2 - 7 + 6
#1. 87 / 3 = 29
#2. 29 * 2 = 58
#3. 58 + 6 = 64
#4. 64 - 7 = 57
print ("89/3*2-4+6=", x)

#Example 2
x = 9 + 5 / 3 * 3
#1. 9 / 3 = 3
#2. 3 * 3 = 9
#3. 9 + 5 = 14
print ("9+5/3*3=", x)

#Example 3
x = 12 % 2 + 8 / 2 * 3
#Explain how this operation is carried out and
check your answer
print ("12%2+8/2*3=", x)

#Example 4
x = (8 - 12) - 10 * 4
#Explain how this operation is carried out and
check your answer
print ("(8-12)-10*4=", x)

#Example 5
x = 21 / 3 % 4 * 2 ** 3
#Explain how this operation is carried out and
check your answer
print ("21/3%4*2**3=", x)
```

3.3 Output: Printing to the screen

The most straightforward way to output information is by using the print() statement which passes none to multiple expressions separated by commas or combined by a plus sign (+). This statement converts expressions into a string and displays the result as a standard output like this:

Ex9

```
#Ex9

print ("Python is an amazing language, isn't it?")


string1 = "yes"

string2 = "it is"


print (string1, string2, ".")

print (string1+string2+".")
```

When you run this script, this is what will be displayed on your terminal screen:

```
c:\Python35-32\Exfiles>python Ex90.py

Python is an amazing language, isn't it?

yes it is .

yesit is.
```

Have you noticed any difference in how the output is spaced when you use comma or + to combine strings of text?

Hour 4: If-Statements

When you need a program you are writing to do something 20 times, you will not force the user to repeat instructions 20 times, you use iteration. When you write code that tells the computer to repeat a bit of code between two points until a certain condition is met, it is called iteration. We have the If statement in a previous exercise, but we will use it again to understand what it does and how.

Ex10

```
#Ex10

#This is a program to determine which fruits are
more based on user input.

oranges = int(input("Enter the number of mangoes:
"))

apples = int(input("Enter the number of apples:
"))


if oranges < apples: #Checks if oranges are fewer
than apples

     print ("There are more apples than
oranges.")


if oranges > apples: #Checks if oranges are more
than apples

     print ("There are more oranges than
apples.")


if (oranges == apples): #Checks if the number of
apples and oranges are th

     print ("There are as many oranges as
apples.")
```

4.1 Decision making

A computer program is essentially a set of instructions that guide it from the start to finish. Introducing an IF statement alters the linear start-to-finish plot of the program, allowing the program to make decisions and change the way it works. Here is a graphical representation of how the If statement affects how your code runs:

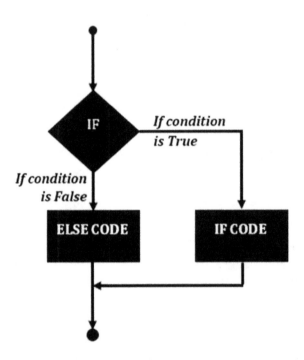

Fig 4: If decision flow chart

Ex11

Here is a simple exercise to determine whether a number a user enters is positive or negative.

```
#Ex11

num = int(input("Enter a positive or negative
number: "))


if num > 0:

        print ("The number is a positive number!")

if num < 0:

        print ("The number is a negative number!")
```

This if statement includes a Boolean text condition expression. If the result of the test returns true, the print block of code is executed. If the test returns a false, the block is ignored.

4.2 Single IF Statement

If you write a block of code that consists of only one IF, it is acceptable to put the code condition in the same line as the header statement. For example:

```
num = 100

if (num == 100): print ("The value of num is 100!")
```

4.3 If... Else

We can use If...Else when we need to have a block of code executed even when the Boolean test returns a negative. In Exercise 12, you will see how the block of code is executed as presented in fig 4.

Ex12

```
#Ex12

#Program to determine the rate of discount based
on price

price = int(input("Enter the price of the item:
"))


if price < 100:

        discount = (price * 0.05)

        print ("The discount is ", discount)

else:

        discount = (price * 0.1)

        print ("The discount is ", discount)


print ("You will pay ", price - discount, "in
total.")
```

In this exercise, the program asks the user to enter the price of an item then calculates the discount it qualifies for based on the price (5% for items worth less than 100 and 10% for the rest) then displays the discount and the final price of the item.

4.4 Elif

A step from the If...The Else statement is Elif. As you may have guessed already, Elif is essentially a combination of Else and If in one statement. This statement allows the program to check multiple expressions and executes a block of code when one of the conditions returns TRUE. If all the conditions are FALSE, the block will be ignored. Unlike If... Else which can only have one statement, Elif allows an arbitrary number of Elif statements following If.

Ex13

```
#Ex13

#Program to determine the rate of discount based
on price

price = int(input("Enter the price of the item:
"))


if price < 100:

     discount = (price * 0.05)

     print ("The discount is ", discount)


elif price < 500:

     discount = (price * 0.1)

     print ("The discount is ", discount)


elif price < 1000:

     discount = (price * 0.2)

     print ("The discount is ", discount)


else:

     discount = (price * 0.25)

     print ("The discount is ", discount)


print ("The final price of the item is ", price -
discount)
```

4.5 Nested IF Statements

In situations where you want to write a program that checks for another condition after a condition is resolved to true, you can use a nested IF construct. The nested if has the If... Elif.... Else construct within another If... Elif... Else construct.

Ex14

```
#Ex14

#A program to check if a number is divisible by 3 and 2

num = int(input("Enter a number to check divisibility: "))


if num % 2 == 0:

        if num % 3 == 0:

                print ("Divisible by 2 and 3")

        else:

                print ("divisible by 2 not by 3")

else:

        if num % 3 == 0:

                print ("divisible by 3 not by 2")

        else:

                print ("not Divisible by 2 not by 3")
```

Run the code above to understand how this happens.

Hour 5: Loops

In the last chapter, we saw how the If statement could be an incredibly useful tool for programmers. However, the If statement and its variations have a problem in that they are a one-time operation statements. As an example, imagine a password entry screen. When an If is used, the user can only enter a correct or incorrect password without the option to return to the previous screen if the password is wrong.

Loops have almost the same type of functionality as the If statements except with the advantage of being able to repeat until you break the cycle. In the example above, with a good loop statement, the user should be taken back to the password screen when they enter an incorrect password instead of just ending. A loop can take the user back to the input statement to start a process over.

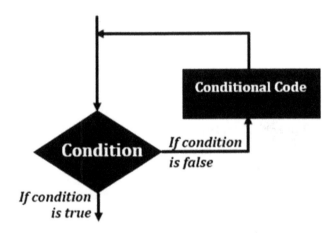

Fig 5: Loop

5.1 The while loop

A while loop statement repeatedly executes a statement or a block of indented code as long as a given condition is true.

Let us begin this section with a simple program. Write the following code and run it, then try to understand what is happening:

Ex15

```
#Ex15

x = 0


while (x < 10):
    x = x + 1
    print (x)
```

You should see a result like this:

```
1

2

3

4

5

6

7

8

9

10
```

What this short code does is explained in this text box:

```
x = 0 #x now equals 0


while (x < 10):    #As long as the value of x is
less than 10, do this:

    x = x + 1      #Add 1 to the value of x

    print (x)      #Display the new value of x and
return to first indent.
```

To put it in a simple language you will remember, this is how you write the While loop:

```
while [enter the condition that the loop
proceeds]:

        [what is done in the loop]

        [what is done in the loop]

[the code here will not be looped because it is
not indented.]
```

Ex16

```
#Ex16

#Countdown from x to 0


x = int(input("Enter a value between 1 and 10: "))


while x != 0:

    print (x)

    x = x - 1

    print ("The countdown is at ", x)
print ("Countdown ended at 0")
```

Test: Use # comments to explain what each line of the code above does.

5.1.1 Else Statement with While

The Else that we used with IF statement is also supported when working with loops. When the Else statement is used with the While loop, the statement after it is excluded when the statement becomes false.

In the next test, you will use Else with the While statement to understand how it works.

Ex17

```
#Ex17

#Countdown from any number greater than 3

x = int(input("Enter a number greater than 3: "))


while x > 3:

    x = x - 1

    print ("The count is ", x)

else:

    print ("The count is less than 3")
```

It is advisable that you use the while loop sparingly while developing Python programs. The for loop that we will look at next is the most preferred loop to use in most situations.

5.2 The for loop

The `for` loop requires some repeatable objects like a set or list to execute a sequence of statements and abbreviate the code that handles the loop variable.

Example:

```
x = range (0, 10)

for count in x:

    print (count)
```

The output of this code will look a lot like that in Ex14, yet the program code is very different. The first line introduces the range function which uses two arguments in the `format range(start, finish)` with start and finish being the first and last numbers in range.

Another way we could have written that code is:

```
for x in range(10):

    print (x)
```

The `range()` function allows the program to access a set of items efficiently. It executes a loop that runs a fixed number of times when used with `the for` statement. When the Start value is not declared, the program index begins at 0.

Ex18

```
#Ex18

fruits = ["Apples", "Mangoes", "Peaches",
"Oranges", "Bananas"]


for fruit in fruits:

        print (fruit)
```

As we saw earlier, the for is an iterator based loop that steps through items in a list, tuples, string, or dictionary keys and other iterable. In this case, the program assigns the list in fruits variable indexes beginning at 0 and follows a sequence of the items in this syntax:

```
for <variable> in <sequence>:

        <statements>
```

5.2.1 Else Statement with For Loop

Just like with the while loop, we can use else with the for loop. In this case, the else statement is executed when the for loop has exhausted iterating the list of items. Note that the else statement in the for loop is only executed when the for loop terminates normally and not when it encounters a break (discussed below).

The syntax takes this form:

```
for <variable> in <sequence>:

        <statements>

else:

        <statements>
```

Ex19

```
#Ex19

numbers=[1,3,45,49,48,69,37,21,71,41,31]


for num in numbers:

     if num %2 == 0:

          print ("The list contains an even
number")

          break

else:

     print ("The list does not contain even
numbers")
```

Find out what happens when you edit out the even number 48in the numbers list above and run the code.

The program should display "The list does not contain even numbers."

5.4 Loop Control Statements

When you want to change execution from a normal sequence in a loop, you use loop control statements. Python supports pass, break, and continue loop control statements. Let us explore what purpose each of these statements serves.

5.4.1 Pass statement

When a statement is required to syntactically change the execution of a loop without the use of code or command, the pass statement is what you would use. It is a null operation, which means that nothing happens when it is executed. The pass statement is very useful in situations where the code will eventually go but has not yet been written.

Ex20

```
#Ex20

numbers = [3,5,2,7,0,4,3,8,10]

for number in numbers:

        if number == 0:

                pass

                print ("Pass 0")

        print ("Current number is: ", number)

print ("Bye!")
```

5.4.2 Break statement

The break statement terminates the loop and transfers the next execution to the statement immediately following the loop. This statement is used for premature termination of a loop. After the loop is abandoned, the execution of the next statement is resumed.

Here is a flow diagram showing how the broken syntax works in Python.

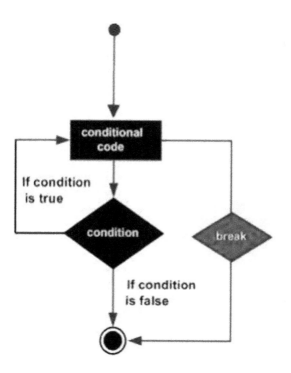

Fig 6

The most common use of the break statement us when an external condition that requires a hasty exit is triggered. The break statement, used in both `for` and `while` loops, also stops the execution of the innermost loop in a nested loop and begins executing the next line following the block of code.

Ex21

```
#Ex21

age = int(input("How old are you? "))

dob = 2017 - age

counter = 1


while age < 0 or age >130:

     print ("Attempt {0}: Age not
valid.".format(counter))

     age = int(input("How old are you? "))

     counter = counter + 1

     if counter >=5:

          age = 0

          break
print ("You used {0} chances to enter your
age.".format(counter))

if age == 0:

     print ("You have failed to enter a valid
age.")

else:

     print ("You are aged {0}. You were born in
".format(age), dob )
```

In this exercise, the program expects the user to enter his/her age in years and only allows five attempts. The age must be between 0 and 130. The counter records the number of invalid entries, and when it gets to 5, it sets the age as 0 and breaks the loop. When the loop is broken, the very next print statement. If the circuit is not broken, the block after else is run.

5.4.3 Continue statement

The continue statement causes the loop to skip the remaining part of the block of code and immediately retests the condition before the reiteration.

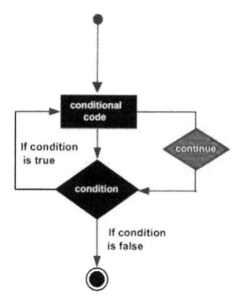

Fig 7

This statement can be used in both for and while loops.

```
#Ex22

while True:

        num = int(input("Enter a positive number to
proceed or 0 to exit: "))

        if num < 0:

                print ("Please enter a positive number
only.")

                continue

        elif num == 0:

                print ("Exiting program...")

                break

        num_cube = (num ** 3)

        print ("The cube of {0} is {1}.".format
(num, num_cube))

print ("Operation completed.")
```

This exercise combines the `continue` and `breaks` loop control expressions, albeit in different blocks of code. Can you explain what they do?

5.5 Indentation

For a code you write to be executed right, all the conditions must be met, including proper indentation. This is particularly important when it comes to loops and iteration. For instance, to loop five lines of code using the while loop, all the five lines must be indented by four spaces or one tab about the beginning of the loop statement. This is a vital programming practice no matter what language you use. Python requires that you properly indent your code. In the example below, notice how uniform the indentation is and try to figure out which lines are related.

Ex23

```
#Ex23

x = int(input("Enter a number to test: "))


while x > 0:

    print (x)

    if x > 5:

        print ("The number is greater than 5.")

    elif x % 2 == 0:

        print ("This is an even number.")

        print ("It is also 5 or smaller.")

    else:

        print ("This number is greater than
5.")

        print ("It is also an odd number.")

    x = x - 1

    print ("The value of x is now less by 1.")

print ("The number is greater than 0!")
```

Hour 6: Functions

If you are new to software development, you will be surprised by just how much source code of a program is general and re-used. Copy-pasting is a very common practice in programming because many functions are similar in different programs. These include verifying that certain numbers or data types are acceptable if a string fits a particular requirement, or that a print statement works well with a general data structure.

In python, the section of code you would copy whole because it runs independently is called a function. We can define a function as a block of organized and reusable code that performs a single distinct but related action. Functions make your code modular and reusable. Python provides a built-in function such as `print` (""), but you will also learn to create yours, called `user-defined functions`.

6.1 Defining a Function

Here are five simple rules you must follow when defining functions in Python:

1. A function block begins with the keyword def followed by the name of the function and parentheses ().

2. The first statement in a function can be an optional statement such as doc string or the documentation string of the function.

3. The code block within the function is indented and begins with a colon (:)

4. Use return [expression] to exit a function, with the option to pass back the expression to the caller.

5. If the function has arguments or input parameters, they should be placed within the parentheses. Parameters can also be defined inside the parentheses.

Without specifying functions, your code would be very repetitive and clumsy. Programmers hate to repeat things, and considering computers were made just to handle repetitive tasks; it is expected that you use functions to minimize it.

Syntax

```
def functionname(parameters):

    "function_docstring"

    function_suite

    return [expression]
```

Parameters have a positional behavior by default and should be informed in the same order they are defined.

```
numbers = input("Enter two numbers separated by a comma: ")

list = numbers.split(",")

highest = max (list)

print ("The highest value is ", highest)
```

In Ex24, we use an inbuilt function called `max` that finds the maximum value from two or more numbers. This program asks the user to enter several numbers separated by commas then creates a `list` out of them. The `max` function finds the maximum number and assigns variable `highest` before displaying it.

Our task is to define our function to replace Max. We will call it `MyMax`.

```
#Ex24

def MyMax (firstnumber, secondnumber):

    if firstnumber > secondnumber:

        return firstnumber

    else:

        return secondnumber


numbers = input("Enter two numbers separated by a
comma: ")

list = numbers.split(",")


firstnumber = list[0]

secondnumber = list[1]


result = MyMax(firstnumber, secondnumber)

print (result, "is the greater of the two
numbers.")
```

6.2 Calling a Function

When you define a function, you give it a name and specify the
parameters that are required for the function and the structures of
code. After you finalize the basic structure of the function, you will

be able to execute it by calling it directly from the Python prompt or another function.

Ex25

```
#Ex25

def cubed(x):

    y = x ** 3

    return y


a = int(input("Enter a number to cube: "))

result = cubed(a)

print ("The result of ", str(a), " cubed is ",
str(result))
```

In Ex25, just after the return statement, the program asks the user to enter a number to find a cube for. The number a is 'cubed 'as per the cubed function we defined and its result, which is represented by y in the Function, is printed out as a string.

You can substitute the expression return with any Python expression and even avoid creating the variable y to represent the answer to leave on return x ** 3 and the program will work just the same (try it). However, it is a good programming practice to use temporary variables such as y in our defined function to make it easy to debug the program later. Such temporary variables are called *local variables*.

6.3 Time-saving functions

One of the best things about functions is that they make it possible (and easier) to write an efficient code that you can use again and again. For instance, if you write a function that verifies data a user enters, you can use it in the future when you create a program that requires this function to work.

Before you create a function, you should first find out what its inputs and outputs are. In our case, we know that the user enters an integer as input and gets the output as a string of the cubed number. If our function were efficient enough, it would also verify that the right data is entered (for instance entering alphabetical characters will cause a ValueError.

When you create a function, the best way to make it of most value is to make it time-saving. This means you should be able to tweak the function slightly, if at all when you want to fit it in another code in the future.

6.4 Pass by reference vs. value

One thing that makes how Python treats function parameters different from standard variables is that its function parameters are passed by value. All parameters (arguments) in Python are passed by reference meaning that when the value of a parameter the function refers to changes, the change will also be reflected in the calling function. Function parameters are sacred. When a parameter refers to an integer, the function provides a copy of the value of the variable, not access to the variable itself. Let us look at how this works in Ex26.

Ex26

```
#Ex26

def listchange(fruits):

    "This changes the list to this function."

    print ("Parameter values before change: ",
fruits)

    fruits[2] = "Vegetable"

    print ("Parameter values after change: ",
fruits)

    return


#Now to call the listchange function


fruitslist = input("Enter fruit names separated by
commas: ")

fruits = fruitslist.split(",")

listchange(fruits)


print ("Values outside function: ", fruits)
```

Here is what you should see when you run Ex26. In this demo, I used examples Apple, Mango, Peach, and Orange.

```
C:\Python35-32\Exfiles>python ex26.py

Enter fruit names separated by commas: Apple, Mango, Peach, Orange

Parameter values before change: ['Apple', ' Mango', ' Peach', ' Orange']

Parameter values after change: ['Apple', ' Mango', 'Vegetable', '
Orange']

Values outside function: ['Apple', ' Mango', 'Vegetable', ' Orange']
```

In this demonstration, we have maintained the reference of the passed object while appending a value in the same object. You will notice that the function modifies the third item in the list by replacing it with "Vegetables," value that is retained outside the function.

Ex27

Let us do another example where an argument is passed by reference, and the reference overwritten inside the function.

```
#Ex27

def AgeChanger(ages):

    "This changes a passed list to this
function"

    ages = [18,21,34] # This assigns new
references to ages

    print ("Values inside the function: ", ages)

    return


#Now call the AgeChanger function

ages = [10,15,20]

AgeChanger(ages)

print ("Values outside the function: ", ages)
```

When you run this exercise, you should see something like this:

```
C:\Python35-32\Exfiles>python Ex27.py

Values inside the function:  [18, 21, 34]

Values outside the function:  [10, 15, 20]
```

The parameter `ages is` local to the function `AgeChanger`. When you change ages within the function, it does not affect ages outside the function, therefore producing nothing.

6.4 Function Arguments

There are several ways you can call a function. You can use the following formal argument types:

- Required arguments
- Keyword arguments
- Default arguments
- Variable-length arguments

6.4.1 Required arguments

These are arguments that are passed to a function in their correct positional order. The number of arguments in the function call must be an exact match with the function definition. Here is a good example.

```
def DisplayMe(str):

    "This prints a passed string into this
function"

    print (str)

    return


#Now  can call DisplayMe function

DisplayMe()
```

When you run the example above, you will encounter an error because you have to pass one argument:

```
TypeError: DisplayMe() missing 1 required
positional argument: 'str'
```

6.4.2 Keyword arguments

Keyword arguments are closely related to function calls. When a keyword argument is used in calling a function, the caller identifies the arguments by the name of the parameter. This makes it possible for you to place arguments out of order or skip them because the interpreter can use the keywords provided to match parameters with values. For instance, we could call the DisplayMe() function like this:

```
def DisplayMe(str):

    "This prints a passed string into this function"

    print (str)

    return


# Now call the DisplayMe function

DisplayMe(str = "Display text.")
```

When you run this code, you will see:

```
Display text.
```

To explain this better, we will do an exercise. Keep in mind the order of parameters to see if it matters.

Ex29

```
#Ex29

def showinfo(name, sex):

    "This prints a passed info into the function"

    print ("Name: ", name)

    print ("Sex :", sex)

    return


#Now call the showinfo function

showinfo(sex = "male", name = "John" )
```

When the Ex30 code is executed, you should see a result like this:

```
C:\Python35-32\Exfiles>python Ex29.py

Name:    John

Sex:   male
```

As you can see, the order of the parameters does not matter when the keyword is used when calling an argument.

6.4.3 Default arguments

A default argument can be defined as an argument that assumes the default value when it is not provided in the function call for the argument. In Ex30, the default age and name argument values are used if not passed.

```
#Ex30

def showinfo (name = "Null", age = 20):

    "This prints a passed information into the
function"

    print ("Name: ", name)

    print ("Age: ", age)

    return


showinfo(age = 31, name = "Moses")

showinfo(name = "Sarah")  #Default age argument will
be used

showinfo(age = 26)        #Default name argument
will be used
```

Can you identify situations where default arguments are necessary for Ex30?

6.4.4 Variable-length arguments

A variable-length argument comes in handy when you need to process a function with more arguments than specified in the function definition. Unlike the required and default arguments, the variable-length arguments are not named in the function definition.

The syntax of a function with one-keyword variable arguments looks like this:

```
def function_name([formal_args,] *
var_args_tuple):

        "function_docstring"

        function_suite

        return [expression]
```

An asterisk (*) is inserted before the variable name that will hold the values of the non-keyword variable arguments. The variable arguments tuple will remain empty if no new arguments are specified when the function is called.

6.5 The returnStatement

The statement `return [expression]` that we have used throughout this chapter exits the function. A return statement that has no arguments is similar to return None. Ex31 is an example of a function that returns a value.

Ex31

```
#Ex31

def multiply(arg1, arg2):

    "Multiply the parameters and return the
product."

    product = arg1 * arg2

    print ("Inside the function: ", product)

    return product


x = int(input("Enter the first number: "))

y = int(input("Enter the second number: "))

#Nowcall the multiply function

answer = multiply(x, y)

print ("Outside the function : ", answer)
```

Hour 7: Dictionaries

Think of a traditional dictionary – the book that provides the definition of English words. The words and their definitions are indexed together in one document, more like a list. Each word and its definition make up a string. The idea behind dictionaries in Python is a lot like this.

On a traditional dictionary, the first word and its definition *"a: The first letter of the alphabet"* could be assigned index 0 in Python. When referencing a word in the book dictionary, we typically search for a word based on an alphabetical index where instead of searching for index 0 to find the definition of "a," we could refer to it as "index a." Instead of looking at index 0 in the dictionary to find what we want, we look for index a. Instead of `dictionary[0]`, we use `dictionary["a"]`. Get it?

7.1 Keys and Values of the Dictionary

The idea behind the dictionary in Python is to retrieve values based on more meaningful keys rather than just use a collection of numbers. Dictionaries are in many cases more useful to use than lists, which use numerical indexes to provide access to values. Note, though, that both lists and dictionaries are very helpful in different cases, but you must know their differences to apply them right.

The key and the value of a dictionary is separated by a colon (:), the items are separated by commas (,), and the whole dictionary is enclosed in curly braces ({}). A dictionary called MyDict would look like this:

```
MyDict = {'Name': 'Waldo', 'Age': 25, 'Sex':
'Male', 'Location': 'Italy'}
```

You can also create a dictionary that looks like this:

```
MyDict = {

'Name': 'Waldo',

'Age': 25,

'Sex': 'Male',

'Location': 'Italy'

}
```

In a dictionary, keys must be unique while values may not. Keys must also be of immutable data types such as numbers, strings, or tuples but values may not

7.2 Accessing Values in Dictionary

You are already familiar with how to access values in a list using square brackets enclosing an index value, accessing dictionary elements should be a piece of cake because they are pretty much the same thing. Here is a simple example on how to access values in a dictionary:

Ex32

```
#Ex32

MyDict = {'Name': 'Waldo', 'Age': 25, 'Sex': 'Male',
'Location': 'Italy'}

print ("I am", MyDict['Name'], "aged",
MyDict['Age'], "from", MyDict['Location']+".")
```

Write the above code in your text editor and run it. You should see something like this:

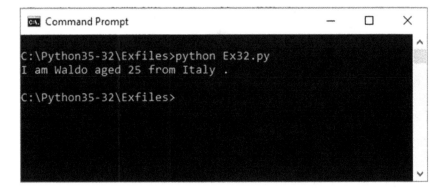

```
Command Prompt                          —    □    ×

C:\Python35-32\Exfiles>python Ex32.py
I am Waldo aged 25 from Italy .

C:\Python35-32\Exfiles>
```

What happens when you try to access a data item using a key that is not included in the dictionary? Let us try it with the example above and see what error we get.

```
#Ex32

MyDict = {'Name': 'Waldo', 'Age': 25, 'Sex':
'Male', 'Location': 'Italy'}

print ("I am", MyDict['Name'], "a",
MyDict['occupation'], "from",
MyDict['Location']+".")
```

You should get the error `KeyError: 'occupation'` when you run the code above. This essentially means that the key is not existent.

7.3 Updating the Dictionary

You can update the dictionary by adding new entries or key-value pairs or modifying or deleting existing entries. In Ex33, we will put each of these in practice to understand how they work.

76

7.3.1 Modifying Dictionary Elements

Ex33

```
#Ex33

MyDict = {'Name': 'Waldo', 'Age': 25, 'Sex':
'Male', 'Location': 'Italy'}


name = str(input("Enter a new name: "))

age = int(input("Enter your age: "))

location = str(input("Where are you? "))


MyDict['Name'] = name

MyDict['Age'] = age

MyDict['Location'] = location


print ("The new user is", MyDict['Name'], "aged",
MyDict['age'], "from", MyDict['Location']+".")
```

This shortcode has a dictionary with four keys with paired values. It prompts the user for new values stored in variables called name, age, and location then assigns them to the 'Name,' 'age,' and 'Location' keys of the MyDict dictionary.

Can you modify the code to allow the user to enter a new string and modify the 'Sex' value in the dictionary?

7.3.2 Deleting Dictionary Elements

There are functions that you can use to remove the elements of a dictionary individually or erase all the contents at once. You can also use `del.dict` to delete the entire dictionary. Note that when you delete the dictionary, any references to it or its keys and values will return an exception because the dictionary will no longer exist.

Ex34

```
#Ex34

MyDict = {'Name': 'Waldo', 'Age': 25, 'Sex':
'Male', 'Location': 'Italy'}


print ("List of keys before
deletion:",list(MyDict.keys()))


del MyDict['Location']


print ("List of keys after deletion:",
list(MyDict.keys()))
```

This code will give you a `KeyError: 'Location'` when you run it because `'Location'` has been removed.

To clear all the entries in the dictionary, `dict.clear()`.

7.4 Properties of Dictionary Keys

There are no restrictions as far as using dictionary values goes. You can use arbitrary objects including standard and user-defined objects. However, when it comes to keys, there are two important rules you must always remember as I mentioned in the introduction:

1. Keys must be unique. You cannot have more than one similar keys in a dictionary.
2. Keys are immutable. You cannot use something like [key] to define a key.

7.5 Built-in Dictionary Functions and Methods

In this section, I will go through a list of the essential functions and approaches built into Python that you can use with dictionaries. I suggest that you study the description of the different methods and functions and apply them to Ex36 then run the code to see what they do.

Ex35

```
#Ex35

GradsList = {'StudentID': 200627,'FirstName':
'Alison','LastName': 'Fairbanks','Email':
'afairbanks@email.com','DOB': 1995,'Sex':
'F','Major': 'Music','Faculty': 'Arts',}
```

For example, to try the `len(GradsDict)` function, first understand what it does, find out what the output should be, then enter this in your Ex35.py code:

```
#Ex35

GradsDict = {'StudentID': 200627,'FirstName':
'Alison','LastName': 'Fairbanks','Email':
'afairbanks@email.com','DOB': 1995,'Sex':
'F','Major': 'Music','Faculty': 'Arts',}


print ("len(dict):", len(GradsDict))
```

Function	Description
len(GradsDict)	This is the length function which gives the number of items in the dictionary.
str(GradsDict)	This gives a printable string representation of the dictionary.
type(variable)	Gives the type of the passed variable. For a dictionary, it returns dictionary type.

Method	Description
GradsDict.clear( )	Removes all the elements in the dictionary including keys and values.
GradsDict.copy()	Makes a shallow copy of the GradsDict dictionary
GradsDict.fromke ys()	Creates a new dictionary with the GradsDict keys.
GradsDict.get(ke y, default=None)	For the specified key (e.g.) 'email', returns value. If no value is assigned, it returns default.
GradsDict.items( )	Returns the GradsDict(key, value) tuple pairs as a list.
GradsDict.keys()	Returns a list of the GradsDict keys.

`GradsDict.setdefault(key, default=None)`	Similar to get() except that it sets the `GradsDict[key]` to default if it is not in the dictionary already
`GradsDict.update(GradsDict2)`	Takes the key-value pairs of `GradsDict2` and adds them to `GradsDict`
`GradsDict.values()`	Returns the values of `GradsDict` dictionary.

Hour 8: Classes

In the introduction to this book, we described Python as an Object Oriented Programming language. This is because Python lets you structure your code in a way that uses modules, classes, and objects with ease. This chapter focuses on helping you master Python's object-oriented setup to create a consistent program that can be run in a 'cleaner' way. You will find out what objects in programming are and how modules and classes are used.

If you find it difficult to grasp these full, do not worry because everyone new to programming struggles at first to understand the plain weird set up that is OOP. In the conclusion of this book, you will find a few recommendations of web resources you can refer to understand the in-depths of OOP fully.

8.1 Overview of Terminologies used inOOP

Class: This is a prototype for an object defined by the user with attributes that characterize an object. The characteristics, in this case, include data members (instance and class variables) and methods.

Object: An object is made up of data members including class variables and instance variables as well as methods that create a unique instance of a data structure defined by its class.

Data member: This is an instance variable or a class variable that stores the data associated with an object and its class.

Class variable: This is a variable that is shared by all the instances of a class. It is defined within a class but outside of any of the class's methods.

Instance variable: This is a variable defined inside a method. An instance variable belongs only to the current class instance.

Instance: An object of a particular class also defined as an object that belongs to a class Circle.

Instantiation: The process of creating an instance of a class.

Inheritance: Inheritance is the process of transferring the characteristics of class to other classes derived from the parent class.

Method: A special form of the function defined within a class definition.

Function overloading: This is when you assign more than one behavior to a function. Function overloading varies with the types of arguments and objects involved.

Operator overloading: This is when more than one function is assigned to an operator.

8.2 Creating Classes

To put it in a way that is easy to understand, a class is a kind of container where you will group all related data and functions to be able to access using a "." (dot) operator.

A new class definition is created using the class statement followed by the name of the class then a colon, like this:

```
class ClassName:

    "class documentation string"

    class_suite
```

The class can also have an optional documentation string right below the definition as shown above and can be accessed using `ClassName._doc_`.

The `class_suite` contains all the basic statements that define the class members, functions, and data attributes.

Ex36

```
#Ex36

class MyContacts:

        "Details of my contacts"

        ContCount = 0


        def __init__(self, name, number):

                self.name = name

                self.number = number

                MyContacts.ContCount += 1


        def ContactCount(self):

                print ("Total contacts:",
MyContacts.ContCount)


        def ShowContact(self):

                print (self.name, "-", self.number)
```

In this exercise, we have created a class called MyContacts.

- The ContCountvariable is a class variable. Its value is shared with all the instances of the class and can be accessed as `MyContacts.ContCount` within and outside the class.

- The _init_ () method is a unique method also called initialization or the class constructor method. Python calls this method when you create a new instance of the MyContacts class
- The first argument to each method is *self*. All other categories are declared like standard functions. You do not need to add the *self*-argument to the list because Python adds it for you.

8.3 Creating Instance Objects

To create a new instance of a class, first, you call the class using the class name then pass in the arguments that the _init_ method accepts. Let us create an instance object for the class we set up in Ex36. Modify Ex36 by adding the following instance objects:

```
"These create the objects of the MyContacts class"

Contact1 = Mycontacts("Bonny", "0789182733")

Contact2 = MyContacts("Peter", "0739237494")

Contact3 = MyContacts("Janet", "0718297621")
```

Save the new code as Ex37.py. Your exercise code should look like this:

```
#Ex37

class MyContacts:

    "Details of my contacts"

    ContCount = 0


    def __init__(self, name, number):
        self.name = name
        self.number = number
        MyContacts.ContCount += 1


    def ContactCount(self):
        print ("Total contacts:",
MyContacts.ContCount)


    def ShowContact(self):
        print (self.name, "-", self.number)


"These create the objects of the MyContacts
class"
Contact1 = Mycontacts("Bonny", "0789182733")

Contact2 = MyContacts("Peter", "0739237494")

Contact3 = MyContacts("Janet", "0718297621")
```

8.4 Accessing and Working with Attributes

Attributes are accessed using the dot (.) operator with the object. A class variable is accessed using the class name like this: `Contact1.ShowContact()`.

In Ex38, we are going to access the attributes added in Ex37. Modify the Ex37 code again as shown below and save it as Ex38.py then execute it from the terminal.

```
#Ex38
class MyContacts:
      "Details of my contacts"
      ContCount = 0

      def __init__(self, name, number):
            self.name = name
            self.number = number
            MyContacts.ContCount += 1

      def ContactCount(self):
            print ("Total contacts:",
MyContacts.ContCount)

      def ShowContact(self):
            print (self.name, "-", self.number)

"These create the objects of the MyContacts
class"
Contact1 = MyContacts("Bonny", "0789182733")
Contact2 = MyContacts("Peter", "0739237494")
Contact3 = MyContacts("Janet", "0718297621")

Contact1.ShowContact()
Contact2.ShowContact()
Contact3.ShowContact()
print ("Total contacts:", MyContacts.ContCount)
```

If you entered everything right, the result should look something like this:

```
C:\Python35-32\Exfiles>Python Ex38.py

Bonny - 0789182733

Peter - 0739237494

Janet - 0718297621

Total contacts: 3
```

In Ex39, we will practice adding and modifying attributes.

If you entered everything right, the result should look something like this:

```
#Ex39
class MyContacts:
        "Details of my contacts"
        ContCount = 0

        def __init__(self, name, number):
                self.name = name
                self.number = number
                MyContacts.ContCount += 1


        def ContactCount(self):
                print ("Total contacts:",
MyContacts.ContCount)


        def ShowContact(self):
                print (self.name, "-", self.number)

"These create the objects of the MyContacts class"
Contact1 = MyContacts("Bonny", "0789182733")
Contact2 = MyContacts("Peter", "0739237494")
Contact3 = MyContacts("Janet", "0718297621")

print ("Original class attributes:")
Contact1.ShowContact()
Contact2.ShowContact()
Contact3.ShowContact()
print ("Total contacts:", MyContacts.ContCount)

Contact1.name = "Boniface"
Contact2.name = "Nancy"
Contact3.number = "0779204852"
```

Here are the functions you can use to add, modify, and delete attributes:

- `getattr(obj, name[, default])` is used to access the attribute of an object
- `hasattr(obj,name)` is used to check if an attribute exists or not.
- `setattr(obj,name,value)` is used to set an attribute or create one if it does not exist.
- `delattr(obj, name)` is used to delete an attribute.

8.5 Built-In Class Attributes

Every Python class by default has the following attributes built-in and can be accessed using the dot (.) operator just like any other attribute.

`__name__`: Class name.

`__dict__`: Dictionary containing namespace of the class.

`__doc__`: Class documentation string. If undefined, none.

`__module__` ("__main__"in interactive mode): Module name in which the class is defined.

`__bases__`: A tuple containing the base classes arranged in order of occurrence in the base class list. This class could be possibly empty.

Let us used these attributes in the code we saved as Ex 38 to see firsthand what they do. Save the code as Ex40 and run it on the terminal.

```
#Ex40
class MyContacts:
      "Details of my contacts"
      ContCount = 0

      def __init__(self, name, number):
            self.name = name
            self.number = number
            MyContacts.ContCount += 1

      def ContactCount(self):
            print ("Total contacts:",
MyContacts.ContCount)

      def ShowContact(self):
            print (self.name, "-", self.number)

print ("MyContacts.__doc__:",
MyContacts.__doc__)
print ("MyContacts.__name__:",
MyContacts.__name__)
print ("MyContacts.__module__:",
MyContacts.__module__)
print ("MyContacts.__bases__:",
MyContacts.__bases__)
print ("MyContacts.__dict__:",
MyContacts.__dict__)
```

8.6 Class Inheritance

You do not need to create a class from scratch every time. If you can derive it from an existing class, list the parent class in parentheses right after the new class name. The child class will inherit the attributes of the parent class, and you will be able to use its attributes just as if they are defined in the child class. A child class will, however, override any data members and methods from the parent class.

Here is the syntax for class inheritance:

You can also derive a class from two or more parent classes as demonstrated in the syntax above. You can use `isinstance()` or `issubclass()` to check how two classes and instances relate.

- `isinstance(ChildClass, ParentClass)` is a Boolean function that will return true if the given child class is a subclass of the parent class.
- `issubclass(object, class)` is a Boolean function that returns true if the `obj` is an instance of the class or if an instance is a subclass of the `class`.

8.7 Overriding Methods

You can override the parent class methods when working with a child class especially if you want a different or special functionality in the subclass. Here are some of the generic functionalities that you can override in the subclasses:

`__init__ (self [,args...])`: This is a constructor with optional arguments.

`__del__ (self)`: Deletes an object.

`__repr__ (self)`: Represents an evaluable string.

`__str__ (self)`: Represents a printable string.

`__cmp__` `(self, x)`: Used to compare objects.

8.8 Overloading Operators

If your code will at some point add two-dimensional vectors, you could define the _add_ method in the class to handle vector addition to preventing errors. Here is a demo you can try:

Ex41

```
#Ex41

class NumAdder:

  def __init__(self, x, y):

    self.x = x

    self.y = y


  def __str__(self):

    return "NumAdder (%d, %d)" % (self.x,
self.y)


  def __add__(self, z):

    return NumAdder(self.x + z.x, self.y + z.y)


a1 = NumAdder(5, 7)

a2 = NumAdder(-3, 9)

print (a1 + a2)
```

Hour 9: Files and Exceptions

When your program is running, it stores the data it is working with temporarily in the computer's primary memory. This data is lost when the program ends or the computer powers off. The only way to store data permanently is to save it in a file that is stored in the computer's secondary memory which is typically the hard disk.

9.1 Reading and Writing Files

By default, Python offers basic methods and functions a user needs to manipulate files. Most of these file manipulation processes use the file object. The most important commands that you need to understand how they work and know how to use in this section are:

`read()`: Accesses the contents of the file. You will learn to assign the contents of the file to a variable.

`write()`: This method enters data into the file.

`readline()`: Unlike read, this function reads just one line in the text file.

`truncate()`: This command empties the content of a text file. Be careful when using truncate on files with vital data.

`close()`: This closes the file, much like the File > Save process in your text editor/

For the exercises in this hour, we will create a text file in our default save directory (where you save .py files) and give it the name Poem.txt. You can do this right from your text editor.

```
The Dust of Snow


The way a crow

Shook down on me

The dust of snow

From a hemlock tree


Has given my heart

A change of mood

And saved some part

Of a day I had rued.
```

Save the file as *Poem.txt*.

9.1.1 The read() Method

We use read() to read a string of text or binary data from an open file. The syntax for this method takes this format:

```
fileobject = open(file_name, [access_mode],
[buffering])
```

file_name: This string value argument contains the name of the files you want to access.

access_mode: This is an optional parameter that determines the mode in which a file can be opened. The table below summarizes the different modes you should know about.

Mode	Description
r	This is read-only mode. Unless specified, the default mode in which a file is opened is in this mode by default. The file pointer is positioned at the start of the file.
rb	Opens a file in binary format for reading only. The pointer is positioned at the start of the file.
r+	Opens a file for reading and writing in text format. The file pointer positioned at the start of the file.
rb+	Opens a file for reading and writing but in binary format. The file pointer placed at the beginning of the file.
w	Opens a file for writing only and overwrites the file it already exists. If it does not exist a new file for writing is created.
wb	Opens a file for writing only but in binary format and creates one if the file does not exists. Overwrites if the file already exists.
w+	Opens a file ready for reading and writing and overwrites the existing file if it already. If the file does not exist, a new one for reading and writing is created.
wb+	Opens a file in binary format for reading and writing and overwrites the existing one if already exists. If it does not, a new one ready for reading and writing is created.
a	Opens a file in append mode. The pointer is positioned at the end of the file if it exists. If the file does not exist, a new one for writing is created.
ab	Opens a file in binary format in append mode. The pointer is positioned at the end of the file if it exists. If the file does not exist, a new one for writing is created.
a+	Opens a file for reading and appending in the append mode. The file pointer is at the end of the file if it exists. If it does not exist, a one is created for reading and writing.

ab+	Opens a file in binary format for reading and appending in append mode. The pointer is positioned at the end of the file if the file exists. A new file is created for reading and writing in if the file does not exist.

file_name: This string value argument contains the name of the files you want to access.

Buffering: If the value of buffering is set to 0, no buffering will take place. If set to 1, the program performs line buffering when accessing the file. If the buffering value is specified as an integer greater than 1, buffering is performed with the specified buffer size. If the value specified is negative, the system's default buffer size is used.

Ex42

Start a new file on your text file and enter the following code for Ex42:

```
#Ex42

text = open("Poem.txt", "r")

MyPoem = text.read(16); #Reads the first 16 bytes
in the text and assigns variable MyPoem

print ("Read String is:", MyPoem)



text.close() #Closes the opened file
```

Run Ex42 and see what happens. This is what you should see:

```
C:\Python35-32\Exfiles>Python Ex42.py

Read String is: The Dust of Snow
```

When you open a file using Python's inbuilt `open()` function, a file object will be created which you can use to call support methods it is associated with.

9.1.2 The write() Method

When you need to write a string of data into an open file, you use the `write()` method. Note that strings in Python may contain binary data and not just text. You should also remember that this method does not ('\n') character to the end of the string. This character adds a new line to the end of the string such that the next string will be displayed in a new line.

The syntax for `write()` looks like this:

```
fileObject.write(string);
```

```
#Ex43

MyFile = open("MyFile.txt", "w")

MyFile.write("Poem: The Dust of Snow.\nBy Robert
Frost\n");


print ("File created and saved.\n")


MyFile.close() #Close the opened file


MyText = open("MyFile.txt", "r+")

MyPoem = MyText.read(42);


print ("File content: \n" + MyPoem)


MyText.close()
```

The above exercise has two unique processes. Can you identify which one writes the file then closes it and which one opens and prints it show what string was written to the file MyFile.txt?

9.2 File Positions

If you wish to specify where in the file you would like to read or write text, the tell() method will show you the current position in bytes about the beginning of the file.

The seek(offset, [from]) method is then used to change the file position, with the offset argument indicating the number of bytes by which the position is moved. The [from] argument references the position from which the bytes are moved.

If the from argument is set to 0, the beginning of the file will be the reference position, and if it is 1, the current position will be the reference position. If it is set to 2, the end of the file will be the reference position in the method.

Let us try out these file position commands in Ex44 using the *MyFile.txt* file we created in Ex43.

Ex44

```
#Ex44

MyText = open("MyFile.txt", "r+")

text = MyText.read(50)


print ("String content:", text)


position = MyText.tell(); #To check the pointer
position

print ("The current position is", position)


position = MyText.seek(0, 0) #Move the pointer
to the begining of the file

print ("\n New position is", position)


MyText.close()
```

9.3 Renaming and Deleting Files

The OS module of Python offers various methods that you can use to perform various file processing and manipulation operations including renaming and deleting files. However, to call the functions of this module, you will first need to import it using `import os`.

9.3.1 Renaming files using the rename() method

The `rename()` method requires two arguments: the current name of the file to rename and the new filename to rename to. The syntax goes something like this:

filename to rename to. The syntax goes something like this:

```
os.rename(current_filename, new_filename)
```

In Ex45, let us rename the *Poem.txt* file we created to *The Dust of Snow.txt*.

Ex45

```
#Ex45

import os


os.rename ("Poem.txt", "The Dust of Snow.txt")
#Renames the file


MyText = open("The Dust of Snow.txt", "r+") #Open
the renamed file.

text = MyText.read(50)


print (text)
```

9.3.2 Deleting files using the remove() method

The `os.remove()` method is used to delete files. The argument required by the method is the name of the file to be removed. It looks like this:

```
os.remove(file_name)
```

We will go ahead and delete the MyFile.txt file we created in Ex43 in Ex46. If the file no longer exists in your folder, you can create one and give it the exact similar name or only run Ex43.py again to create it.

Ex46

```
#Ex46

import os


os.remove("MyFile.txt")
```

9.4 File and Directory Related Methods

There are countless resources on the internet where you can learn and practice a broad range of methods you can use to manipulate and handle files and directories. These resources cover:

- OS Object Methods: This offers ways to process files and folders (directories).
- File Object Methods: The file object provides many functions used to manipulate files.

When you pursue learning Python beyond this stage, you will learn how to manipulate and work with directories.

Hour 10: Errors and Exceptions

Errors that happen during the execution of program code are called exceptions. To the average software user, an exception is an instance where a program does not conform to the general rule. An error is resolved by saving the status of the execution when the error occurred and interrupted the normal program flow to execute a piece of code or a particular function known as an exception handler. Depending on the type of error encountered, the exception handler can fix the problem encountered and allow the program to resume normal flow or will prompt the user for data or instructions before resumption.

Python comes with two vital tools used to handle any unexpected errors in the code and to debug it: They are:

1. Exception handlers
2. Assertions

When a script in Python raises an exception, it must be handled immediately; otherwise, the program will terminate and quit.

10.1 Exception Handling

In Python, a code that harbors the risk of an exception is embedded in a try block and caught by an except keyword. Python allows you to create a custom exception, even using the raise statement to force a specified exception to occur.

10.1.1 Table of Standard Exceptions

Before we can learn how to use exception handlers to deal with errors in code, let us first discover what the errors we should expect to encounter are and what they mean. You can always refer to this table to find what caused a mistake you encounter.

Exception	Description
Exception	This is the base class for all exceptions.
Attribute Error	This exception is raised by a failure of attribute assignment or reference.
ArithmeticError	This is the base class for all errors in numeric calculation.
StopIteration	Occurs when an iterator's `next()` method does not point to any object.
SystemExit	Exception caused by the `sys.exit()` function.
StandardError	This is the base class for all built-in exceptions except SystemExit and StopIteration.
OverflowError	Encountered when a calculation exceeds the maximum limit for a numeric type.
FloatingPointError	Raised when there is a failure of a floating point calculation.
ZeroDivisonError	Occurs when there is division or modulo by zero on any numeric types.
AssertionError	Occurs when there is a failure of the Assert statement.
EOFError	Raised when the end of file is reached and there is no input from `input()` function.
ImportError	Occurs as a result of an import statement failure.
KeyboardInterrupt	Encountered when the user interrupts the execution of the program execution, often by pressing *Ctrl+C*.
LookupError	This is the base class for all lookup errors.
IndexError	Error occurs when an index is not found in a specified sequence.

KeyError	Occurs when a specified key is not found in the dictionary.
NameError	Occurs when an identifier is not found in a specified namespace.
UnboundLocalError	Occurs when the program tries to access a local variable in a method or function without a value assigned to it.
EnvironmentError	This is the base class for all exceptions occurring outside the Python environment.
IOError	Occurs when an input or output operation fails.
OSError	Triggered by Operating system-related errors.
SyntaxError	Occurs when there is an error in the code syntax.
IndentationError	Caused by improper indentation.
SystemError	Caused by an internal problem with the interpreter.
SystemExit	Encountered when the interpreter is terminated using the `sys.exit()` function.
TypeError	Raised when an operation encounters a data type different from the specified.
ValueError	Encountered when arguments have invalid values specified despite the built-in functions having the right argument types.
NotImplementedError	Triggered when an abstract method that is expected to run in an inherited class is not implemented.

10.1.2 Exception Handling Syntax

If you suspect that a block of code in your script could raise an exception, it is a good practice to place the suspicious code inside a try: block and below it an `except:` statement that will handle the error correctly. The syntax of the code would look something like this:

```
try:

        Enter your code here;

except PossibleException1:

        If there is PossibleException1, then run
this code

except PossibleException2:

        If there is PossibleException2, then run
this code

else:

        If there is no exception then run this
code.
```

Note that:

- A single try: the statement can have one or more except statements. This is important when you are trying to handle possible multiple errors that you suspect your one block of code could rise.
- It is a good practice to provide a generic except clause that handles any and all exceptions.
- The else: clause is optional. Its code executes only when there are no exceptions raised by the try: block code. You can place the code that does not need the protection of the try: block in the else: block.

110

In Ex47, we will try to open the file MyFile.txt which we do not have permission to write, to raise an exception.

Ex47

```
#Ex47

try:

    text = open ("MyFile.txt", "r") #Open the
file in read-only mode

    text.write("We will try to write into the
text file.")

except IOError:

    print ("Error: Cannot write string to
file.")

else:

    print ("String successfully written to
file.")
```

When you run the code above on your terminal, you should see this:

```
C:\Python35-32\Exfiles>python Ex47.py

Error: Cannot write string to file.
```

Now, try eliminating the error by opening the file in read and write mode then run it. What does it print?

Hint: Change "r" to "r+".

Let us try another example. In Ex48, the program expects the user to enter an integer as the value of n. It should generate an error when the input is a string instead. We will raise a ValueError then use the try: exception handling to resolve it.

Ex48

```
#Ex48

while True:

        try:

                n = int(input("Please enter your
age:"))

                break

        except ValueError:

                print ("Your age must be an integer.
Try again.")

    print ("You are aged", n, "years.")
```

This script contains a loop that only breaks when the user enters a valid integer.

If you have a code that must execute whether an exception is raised in the try block or not, you can use the `finally:` clause. The syntax would look like this: use the `finally:` clause. The syntax would look like this:

```
try:

    Enter your code here;

    In case of an exception, this block is
skipped.

finally:

    This block will ALWAYS be executed.
```

Let us write a script example that puts the try: and finally: clauses in use.

Ex49

```
#Ex49

try:

    text = open("MyFile.txt", "w") #Open the file
in write-only mode.

    text.write ("Dust of Snow by Robert Frost")

finally:

    print ("Error: Cannot find the file or read
the data.")
```

Note: You cannot use the else: clause along with the *finally:* clause.

When there is an exception in the try: block, the execution will be passed to the finally: block immediately. The exception will be raised again after all the statements in the finally: block are executed then handled by the except statement if it is present in a following higher layer of the try: then except statement. Let us try it in Ex50 by writing a script that finds the reciprocal of a number entered by the user.

Ex50

```
#Ex50

try:

    x = float(input("Enter a number: "))

    reciprocal = 1.0 / x

except ValueError:

    print ("You did not enter a valid integer
or float.")

except ZeroDivisionError:

    print ("Cannot divide by 0!")

finally:

    print ("This prints whether there is an
exception or not.")
```

10.2 Assertions

In Python, an assertion is a tool that you use to find bugs faster and with less pain. You can turn it on before use and turn it off after you are finished testing your code. It will test an expression and raise an exception if the result is FALSE. It is a good practice to place the assert statement at the beginning of a function to ensure an input is valid and after a function to validate the output.

10.2.1 The asset statement

Python evaluates accompanying expressions to determine if they are TRUE or FALSE when it encounters the assert statement. If the result is false, the AssertionError exception is raised. The syntax for this statement is:

```
assert Expression[Argument]
```

Ex51

```
#Ex51

def CtoF_Converter(Temp):

        "Convert degrees C to F"

#

        assert (Temp >= -273.15), "Cannot be colder
than absolute zero!"

        return 9.0 / 5.0 * Temp + 32


C = float(input("Enter temperature in Celsius: "))

F = CtoF_Converter(C)



print (C, "degrees Celcius is", F, "degrees
Fahrenheit.")
```

If you run the Ex51.py and enter a number less than 273.15, you should encounter an assertion error akin to this:

```
C:\Python35-32\Exfiles>python Ex51.py

Enter temperature in Celsius: -280

Traceback (most recent call last):

  File "Ex51.py", line 17, in <module>

    F = CtoF_Converter(C)

  File "Ex51.py", line 13, in CtoF_Converter

    assert (Temp >= -273.15), "Cannot be colder than
absolute zero!"

AssertionError: Cannot be colder than absolute zero!
```

Hour 11: Testing Your Code

Testing your code is one of the most important steps of developing a functional program. In fact, it is typically considered a good practice to write testing code than running it in parallel to your primary code. This method is widely used by developers across the development sphere as it helps developers define the precise intent of their code and to create software with more decoupled architecture.

11.1 General rules of testing Python code

Here are the ten commandments of testing your code in Python.

1. The testing unit of your code should focus on a tiny bit of functionality and should prove it correct.
2. Each testing unit should be completely independent. It should be able to run alone within the test suite regardless of the order it is called. The `setup()` and `teardown()` methods can be used to load new datasets and cleanup after testing.
3. Always try to make tests run fast to avoid slowing down the entire development. If testing takes longer because of complex data structure it must process, the test units can be run in separate suites.
4. Practice using your tools to run only tests or test cases then runs them when developing functions inside modules frequently, ideally, automatically every time you save your code.
5. Make it a habit of running the full test suite prior to and after every coding session to be sure that noting is broken in the code before starting or and when ending the session.
6. Put in place a hook that runs all tests before pushing the code to a shared depository if working on the collaborative code.
7. If your development session is interrupted, make a point of writing a broken unit test about what you intend to develop next to know where to start when you resume the next session.

8. The first step in debugging your code should be writing a new test that pinpoints the bug. This is not always the easiest thing to do, but this will help you catch those elusive bugs faster and more comprehensively in your code.
9. Write long descriptive names for your testing functions because unlike regular code, and the unit test code is never called explicitly.
10. Every unit test must have a clear purpose of making it helpful. When something goes wrong, or you have to make some changes, you will rely on the testing suite to make modifications or modify certain behaviors.

11.2 unittest

unittest is a test module that comes with the Python standard library. You can create a test case on unittest by subclassing the unittest.TestCase as shown in the Ex52 syntax code below.

```
#Ex52

import unittest


def counter(x):

    return x + 1


class MyTest(unittest.TestCase):

    def test(self):

        self.assertEqual(counter(4), 5)
```

unittest comes with its test discovery capabilities.

11.3 Doctest

A doctest module searches the code for text that looks like interactive sessions in docstrings then executes them to verify that they execute exactly as shown. Unlike proper unit tests, doctests have different uses and are usually not as detailed. Because of this, doctests do not typically catch obscure regression bugs and special cases.

Doctests are however very useful used as expressive documentation of the main use cases of modules and its components. They should, however, run automatically each time a full test suite is run. Here is an example of how a doctest syntax looks like.

```python
def square(x):
        """Return the square of x.
        >>> square(3)
        9
        >>> square(-3)
        9
        """
        return x * x


if __name__ == '__main__':
    import doctest
    doctest.testmod()
```

11.4 Tools

In this section, I will mention several popular testing tools that you will learn to install and use when you get to learning advanced testing of Python code.

11.4.1 py.test

The py.test is an alternative to the standard unittest module that Python comes with. It is a fully-featured and extensible testing tool that has very simple syntax. Creating a test suite using py.test is as easy as writing a module with several functions.

11.4.2 Nose

Nose is a tool that extends unittest so as to make testing code easier. The nose offers automatic test discovery to save the programmer the hassle of having to create test suites manually. It also comes with multiple plugins with extra features such as coverage reporting, test selection, and xUnit compatible test output.

11.4.3 tox

Tox is a versatile tool that you can use to automate the Python test environment management and even test multiple interpreter configurations. This tool lets you configure complex multi-parameter test matrices using a simple ini-style config file.

11.4.4 Unittest2

This is a backport of Python's unittest module. It features an improved API as well as better aassertions over the original unittest.

11.4.5 mock

unittest.mock features many library tools that you can use to test your Python code. Mock allows you to replace parts of the system you are testing with mock objects and test code by making assertions on how they have been used. It is available in the standard Python library starting with Python 3.3.

Hour 12: Conclusion & Further Reading

Over 50 programs of Python written so far since the first Hello World program about 12 hours, ago (hours of study) and you have become an even better and experienced program. If you followed every step of this eBook so far, you have earned the bragging rights to call yourself a programmer. You started from scratch (like everyone should) and perhaps with no prior experience in programming, can now speak regarding functions, classes, IOError, and much more geeky terms.

This short eBook is compressed to keep it concise and practical. You have so far learned how to tell the computer to do all kinds of things, process text, save your information, and saved processes you have personalized to do exactly what you want. The magic has been to learn how to tell the computer what to do, a skill most people still perceive as pure wizardry.

Python's core philosophy is summarized in The Zen of Python, and it paints the colorful rules that govern the language as:

1. Explicit is better than implicit
2. Simply is better than complex
3. Complexly is better than complicated
4. Beautifully is better than ugly
5. Readability counts

As a testament to just how beautiful Python code can be, this is how Ex36 looks on my editor:

```
C:\Python35-32\Exfiles\Ex36.py - Sublime Text                         —    □    ×

File   Edit   Selection   Find   View   Goto   Tools   Project   Preferences   Help

◄ ►    Ex36.py                    ×

1    #Ex36
2    class MyContacts:
3        "Details of my contacts"
4        ContCount = 0
5
6        def __init__(self, name, number):
7            self.name = name
8            self.number = number
9            MyContacts.ContCount += 1
10
11        def ContactCount(self):
12            print ("Total contacts:", MyContacts.ContCount)
13
14        def ShowContact(self):
15            print (self.name, "-", self.number)
16
17    "These create the objects of the MyContacts class"
18    Contact1 = MyContacts("Bonny", "0789182733")
19    Contact2 = MyContacts("Peter", "0739237494")
20    Contact3 = MyContacts("Janet", "0718297621")
21
22    print ("Original class attributes and objects:")
23    Contact1.ShowContact()
24    Contact2.ShowContact()
25    Contact3.ShowContact()
26    print ("Total contacts:", MyContacts.ContCount)
27
28    Contact1.name = "Boniface"
29    Contact2.name = "Nancy"
30    Contact3.number = "0779204852"
31
32    print ("Updated class attributes and objects:")
33    print ("Total contacts:", MyContacts.ContCount)
34    Contact1.ShowContact()
35    Contact2.ShowContact()
36    Contact3.ShowContact()

⊟  Line 1, Column 6                                  Tab Size: 4      Python
```

It is more important now more than ever that you re-visit everything you learned from Hour 1 and practice every day and create much more scripts that do many different things. The internet is full of resources including challenges to create Python scripts that solve all kinds of problems that you can learn from.

You have come this far, and it shows how much passion you have in becoming better at programming, toast yourself but strive to save 100 .py scripts with tens, maybe hundreds of lines of beautiful code over the next week of study. Explore what the world of Python has to offer and be an active member of Github and a StackOverflow.

There are multitudinous ways you can practice and advance your coding skills every day. Every day, thousands of programmers meet on CodeFights and head writing Python code. It has become a large community of upcoming programmers who have turned learning to create solutions to problems we face everyday pillow fights. You can have fun there, or perhaps in the future, you will take a more ambitious approach and get a certification in Python programming from edX and turn it into a career.

Don't forget to get the FREE "Cyberpunk Python Whizz Kit" if you haven't already. This will help you tremendously in getting the most out of this book.

DOWNLOAD THE FREE WHIZZ KIT HERE:

subscribe.cyberpunkuniversity.com

Links

Here are a parting gift and a pointer to the right direction: A list of the most useful resources you should consider checking out. Write a program to save this list and use it every day to find answers you might have about your code. Perhaps someday you will be writing programs for your home devices including the TV and lighting system or you might push the envelope and create apps for your own AI running on a $35 Arduino board.

Good luck.

Tools

1. Python.org.

This is the official website with all the technical details about the Python programming language.

2. Using Algorithms and Data Structures in Python

http://interactivepython.org/runestone/static/pythonds/index.html

3. Python visualizer tool

http://people.csail.mit.edu/pgbovine/python/tutor.html

4. Thonny, Python IDE for beginners.

This one has intuitive features useful for program runtime visualization

http://thonny.org/

5. Python Essential Reference

http://www.worldcat.org/title/python-essential-reference/oclc/288985690

Course

6. Google's Python class

https://code.google.com/edu/languages/google-python-class/

7. MIT's Using Python for Research

https://www.edx.org/course/using-python-research-harvardx-ph526x

8. 6.00.1x: Introduction to Computer Science and Programming Using Python

http://ocw.mit.edu/courses/electrical-engineering-and-computer-science/6-00-introduction-to-computer-science-and-programming-fall-2008/

https://www.edx.org/course/introduction-computer-science-mitx-6-00-1x-9

https://www.class-central.com/mooc/1341/edx-6-00-1x-introduction-to-computer-science-and-programming-using-python

9. uDemy's Learn Python (for Beginners)

Online course

http://www.udemy.com/learning-python-not-the-snake/

Websites and Tutorials

10. Checking interactive learning resource

A creative way to boost your Python skills through interesting tasks.

http://www.checkio.org/

11. Interactive tutorials on Python

This tutorial for beginners has beautiful interactive examples.

http://jwork.org/learn/doc/doku.php?id=python:start

12. ComparingTypes

Learn how Python relates and compares with other languages. How it is similar with its sister Perl, cousin Java, and an overview of how it was a BIG improvement from ABC.

https://wiki.python.org/moin/ComparingTypes

13. Python Programming Tutorials

More Python tutorials.

https://pythonspot.com/

http://thepythonguru.com/getting-started-with-python/

Interactive Tools and Lessons

14. LearnStreet

A free online Python tutorial with practice exercises

http://www.learnstreet.com/

15. Interactive tutorials for scientific programming using Python

Python tutorials in the video.

http://jwork.org/learn/

16. ShowMeDo

http://showmedo.com/videos/python

Over 240 screencasts that reveal the best secrets about Python as the language of the future.

17. Python Bits

A YouTube playlist is covering interesting Python topics. Ideal for beginners and intermediate learners.

https://www.youtube.com/c/ArtheadSe

18. Envato Tuts+

More Python video tutorials

https://code.tutsplus.com/

19. CodeFights

Compete with bots and humans writing problem-solving programs and mastering Python – in real-time.

https://codefights.com/

www.ingramcontent.com/pod-product-compliance
Lightning Source LLC
Chambersburg PA
CBHW071220050326
40689CB00011B/2388